KERALA

KERALA

Text: Ravi Shankar
Photographs: V. Muthuraman

Lustre Press
•
Roli Books

KERALA OVERVIEW

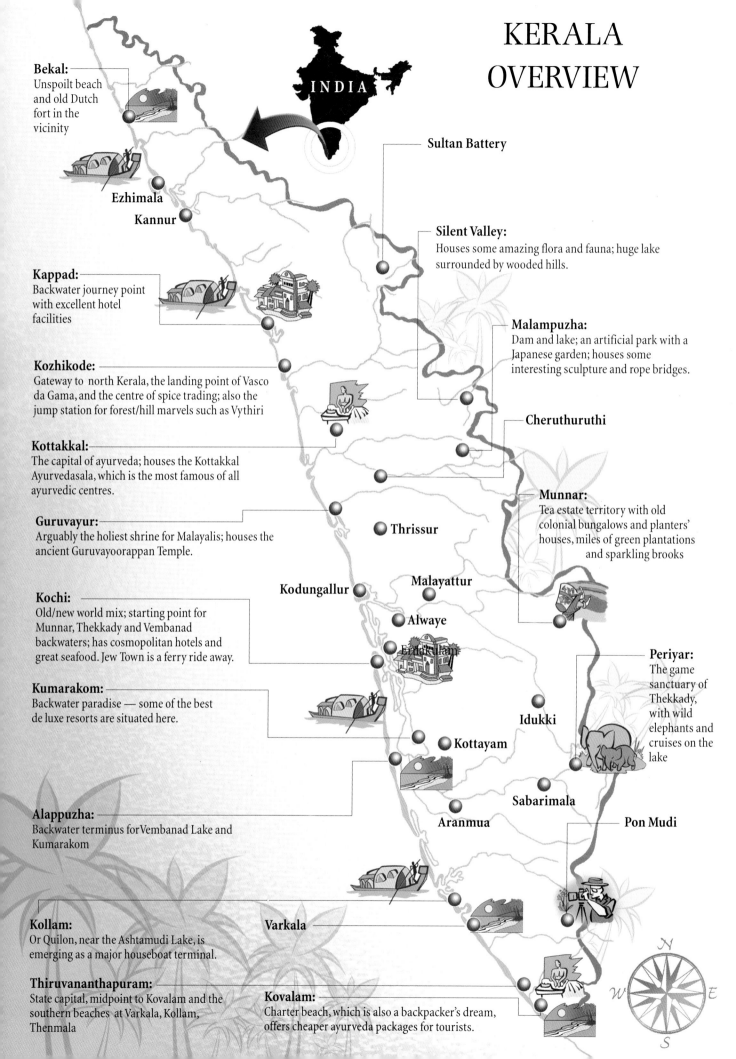

INDIA

Bekal:
Unspoilt beach and old Dutch fort in the vicinity

Ezhimala

Kannur

Kappad:
Backwater journey point with excellent hotel facilities

Kozhikode:
Gateway to north Kerala, the landing point of Vasco da Gama, and the centre of spice trading; also the jump station for forest/hill marvels such as Vythiri

Kottakkal:
The capital of ayurveda; houses the Kottakkal Ayurvedasala, which is the most famous of all ayurvedic centres.

Guruvayur:
Arguably the holiest shrine for Malayalis; houses the ancient Guruvayoorappan Temple.

Kochi:
Old/new world mix; starting point for Munnar, Thekkady and Vembanad backwaters; has cosmopolitan hotels and great seafood. Jew Town is a ferry ride away.

Kumarakom:
Backwater paradise — some of the best de luxe resorts are situated here.

Alappuzha:
Backwater terminus for Vembanad Lake and Kumarakom

Kollam:
Or Quilon, near the Ashtamudi Lake, is emerging as a major houseboat terminal.

Thiruvananthapuram:
State capital, midpoint to Kovalam and the southern beaches at Varkala, Kollam, Thenmala

Sultan Battery

Silent Valley:
Houses some amazing flora and fauna; huge lake surrounded by wooded hills.

Malampuzha:
Dam and lake; an artificial park with a Japanese garden; houses some interesting sculpture and rope bridges.

Cheruthuruthi

Munnar:
Tea estate territory with old colonial bungalows and planters' houses, miles of green plantations and sparkling brooks

Periyar:
The game sanctuary of Thekkady, with wild elephants and cruises on the lake

Thrissur

Malayattur

Kodungallur

Alwaye

Ernakulam

Idukki

Kottayam

Sabarimala

Aranmua

Pon Mudi

Varkala

Kovalam:
Charter beach, which is also a backpacker's dream, offers cheaper ayurveda packages for tourists.

KERALA AT A GLANCE

Transport: Kerala is easily accessible by road, rail and air. The roads are mostly good and places are well connected; modes of transport — trains, buses, taxis, auto rickshaws, bicycles, and in the backwaters, boats.

Best season: The best time of the year to go to Kerala is between October and March.

Accommodation: There is comfortable, clean and readily available accommodation for visitors, ranging from super de luxe to those meant for tourists on a shoe-string budget.

Food: Kerala cuisine is 'finger-lickingly' varied. Coconut and coconut milk are a common base and rice the staple food. Myriad varieties of  fishes, crustaceans, meat, chicken, beef, and vegetarian dishes such as *thoren, avial, olen, kallen, idli, dosa, sambhaar* and *rasam* (to name a few), cooked in uniquely different ways, reflect the state's diverse people and traditions.

Festivals: Hindu, Muslim and Jewish festivals are celebrated with great fervour by all. The most spectacular is Onam, the harvest festival and Malayali New Year. It is celebrated on a grand scale with sumptuous food, floral decorations, folk dances, gifts and boat races.

Handicrafts: Coconut and other fibres are woven into exquisite mats, wall hangings and carpets, and multifarious objects are carved from coconut shells. Buffalo horn, sandalwood and rosewood are crafted into eye-catching objets d'art. Kerala is also famous for its metalware.

Dances: Kathakali, Mohiniattam, Krishnanattam, Theyyam, Kudiyattam and Chavitunatakam weave their magic. Larger than life, dramatic and utterly unforgettable!

Ayurvedic remedial therapy: Oil massages, mud and oil treatment are a part of Kerala's heritage. This therapy has been revived, and now one can join a 'rejuvenation programme', and emerge a new person.

Absolute 'musts': The most famous of the boat races is held on the second Saturday in August in a backwater off Alappuzha. The battle of the 100-oared ram-snouted boats of a bygone age, the *chundan valloms*, is a not-to-be-missed experience.

The Great Elephant March, highlighting many of the festivals in four days, from January 17 to January 20, is specially meant for visitors.

The ancient martial art of *kalaripayattu* has to be seen to be believed.

One can't go to Kerala and not take a boat trip in the backwaters — see and imbibe its serene beauty.

Places to see: Thiruvananthapuram (the capital), the Neyyar Wildlife Sanctuary, Pon Mudi, Kovalam, the beach resort of Varkala, Kollam, Alappuzha, Kochi, Guruvayur, Kodungallur, Kozhikode, Kannur, the Aralam Wildlife Sanctuary, Kottayam, Vembanad Lake, Periyar National Park, Munnar and Thrissur. There is so much more to see and experience. Let your feet wonder off the beaten path and be guided by your spirit and imagination.

Windsong
and
WATER

G o South, until you reach the condyle of the Indian peninsula. That is the point to watch the monsoon coming ashore.

Turn around.

With the sky behind you, stand facing the west. Look at the endless green against the sky. The coconut palms toss their heads in the winds, like Sultans impatient to be rid of their turbans.

Green. Everywhere. The colour of Kerala, a 570-kilometre-long strip of golden, sandy coast on the south-western side of the Indian peninsula, measuring about 120 kilometres at its maximum width and just 30 kilometres at its minimum. Cut off from the rest of India by the mountains of the Western Ghats, its highest point is the summit of Ana Mudi, 2,695 metres above sea level. In the interior, these magnificent mountains contrast with the green valleys. In the west, Kerala is all coastal plains and a shore fringe of sandy beaches and lagoons. Though the state occupies only 1.18 per cent of the land area of India, it contains 3.43 per cent of the country's total population. Between 1961 and 1971, this figure grew by more than 25 per cent. But in the 1970s, the growth was only 19 per cent, a result of an efficient and effective family-planning campaign. About 16 per cent of the people live in the cities, with the rest in large, semi-urban villages or smaller settlements.

The muggy heat of Kerala (which can reach about 34 degrees Celcius) is mitigated to some extent by the rainy season. The monsoon is to Kerala what California's golden

climate is to its people. The rain is a familiar presence, rarely violent and angry, but gentle and revitalising. It contributes to the colours, the scent of verdant vegetation, the tangy sharpness of the paddy winds, the intimate odour of the earth, replete and fulfilled.

*T*he warrior's dance: a kalaripayattu *performance* — kalaripayattu *is known as the earliest form of eastern warfare.*

Pages 14-15: *The mask that is art — a dancer at a Theyyam performance*

Pages 16-17: *Boat racing at Payippad*

Kerala receives two monsoons, first during the summer and later in wintertime. The first showers — *edavappathi* — wash the land by the first of June every year. The season ends by September, when the time is ripe for the annual harvest, celebrated by the Onam festival. The second spate — the north-east monsoon, or *thulavarsham* — begins in

late October and continues into November. The deluge during the month of *Thulam* (mid-October to mid-November) is more dramatic, with evening showers and spectacular thunderstorms. Temperatures go down to a salubrious 18 degrees Celcius.

It is never a good time to drive in Kerala when it is raining. The open spaces make the rain travel in great sheets of white, and sometimes it is like driving through a waterfall. But if you are an automobile lover, October to January is the best time to take to Kerala's roads. They are generally well maintained, though narrower than the highways of North India. The road which Tipu Sultan built — which runs through Malabar — is a black, slim belt of asphalt, winding lazily through the never-ending emerald of paddy fields, bordered by clusters of palm groves and teak, through which the facades of whitewashed old houses peer.

The perennial landscape that unfolds before the wayfarer is one of water and vegetation. You glimpse flashes of the Arabian Sea, its glassy blue flashing at you through coconut groves. Especially as you drive along Kollam, the sea beguiles you with visions of voyages long past — of the early seafaring Moors and Romans, of Vasco da Gama and the great admirals of the Zamorin's fleet.

Kerala has over 100,000 kilometres of paved roads. A national highway and a coastal road connects it with neighbouring states. An extensive rail network runs between the northern border and Thiruvananthapuram, linking main towns such as Ernakulam and Alappuzha. A railway through the Palghat Gap links Kerala to Chennai on India's eastern coast.

Kerala has three major ports — Alappuzha, Kozhikode and Kochi. There are also 10 smaller harbour towns. All these are served by over 1,770 kilometres of inland

Harbour of plenty: Kollam port, which is the heart of the fishing industry.

waterways, used by both humans and freight. Passenger ferries are still a major part of Kerala's transportation system, though freight carriage by canal has declined in importance and yielded to road transport. International airports have been built at Thiruvananthapuram, Kochi and Kozhikode, the three main cities of Kerala. Kochi has a natural harbour. The town has imbibed many cultures and civilisations, through the middle ages into the 19th century — even today Chinese fishing nets billow against the sunset in the Arabian Sea winds. Kochi has a naval base, and the airport there belonged

to the Navy — which has, incidentally, claimed it back after the international airport was opened there.

Even with modern airports, centrally airconditioned shopping malls and luxury hotels, Kerala continues to retain much of its landscape; it has, in fact, so far been impossible to totally change the horizon of the countryside into an urban skyline. The cities of Thiruvananthapuram, Kochi and Alappuzha retain their quaint colours and shapes, along with the sky-rise buildings and apartment complexes that typify modernity. The cities are a charming blend of cultures: colonial buildings with their slim pillars and long verandahs coexist with the gabled *taravadus*. The suburbs are rustic rather than metropolitan — in fact, there is no place in the land which is totally urban. This is ironical, since the people are by and large cosmopolitan!

When it is dusk, on mud and granite platforms, lamps lit to please the snake gods glow and tremble, throwing shadows against gnarled, ancient bark. The stone gods are adorned with sandalwood paste and occult red; and the women bring milk and flowers for the serpentine deities.

The air is spicy with a million scents — there is the fragrance of mango flowers in the breeze, laced with the tang of tamarind, and that of wild flowers growing on the

*S*treet sightings: kitsch on the wall — a poster for a popular jewellery store (above left); a man husking mounds of coconuts at the copra market in Kozhikode (above); an artisan making a replica of a sailing boat in Beypore (right).

*T*he joys of benediction: a mother gets her little son ready for vishukazcha. *Vishu is the festival of spring, and the celebration of plenty. An elaborate vishu altar is prepared lovingly over hours, and the members of the household, starting with the youngest, are woken up at dawn, with their eyes covered, and the altar is revealed in all its blazing glory. Afterwards, they receive gifts from their elders, which is called* vishukkani.

The mascot of the Malayali: elephants are a beloved part of Kerala's history, myth and society, participating in all festivals and auspicious occasions. A mahout washing his pachyderm (above), and another getting his elephant's food ready during a respite at a festival (right).

green hedges of bamboo fences, the odour of vegetation and yesterday's rain, of the blooming jasmine with its compelling redolence, or the ivory-petalled frangipani, which grandmothers say is the favourite abode of the *yakshis* of Kerala — fair, voluptuous vampires with hair like dark forest falls, and eyes luminous with the treacherous secrets of the full moon. Their lips are said to be red like blood, moistened by betel juice.

Myths.

But then, it is a land where time is woven in myth. In its ancient dances — like Kathakali and Theyyam, Mohiniattam and Chakiarkuthu — there is much ornamentation of ritual. Bejewelled with symbolism, artistically fantastic with the use of paint and masks, it is an invitation to look beyond the curtains to another time, another place.

Kerala turns myth into magic, embellishing the fables of India with its own subtleties and craft. It has a stylised artistic tradition; the elaborate symbolism and grammar of Kathakali is no less complicated than the interlayerings of the actual performance. The *ottantullal,* which was the intellectual alternative to Kathakali, is great satirical theatre, created by Kunjan Nambiar in response to the exclusive Brahminical patronage of the older dance traditions of the Namboodris. Kathakali was an exclusive

Jumbo jamboree: At the Thrissur Pooram, hundreds of elephants march in all their caparisoned splendour.

art patronised by the Malayali artistocracy, whose feudal wealth gave them enough leisure for creative appreciation. The festivals were celebrated in temples which were the feudal arenas of dance and culture, where Namboodris and scholars endlessly debated the nuances of *kathakalimudras*, along with the *lakshanas* of elephants. The scene would be magical with light and music: the gigantic, many-tongued *nilavilakkus* lighting up

the night, torches burning in the hands of the serfs, the *nadaswaram* with its haunting
melody, and the *chendas* drumming through the night, as the great elephants, with their
nettipattoms of beaten gold plate stretching down to their tusks, glittering with
diamonds and rubies, nodded, hypnotised by the rhythm, while their mahouts sat
under sequinned silk umbrellas, holding gently swaying peacock fans.

*M*asks of the gods: Kathakali is the most subtle and exquisite performing art to emerge from Kerala (top right). It involves hours of preparation in both make-up and costume. A dancer paints his face (below), after donning the traditional pacha, and another is being painted by trained assistants (bottom right).

Performance has always been the most evident form of expression native to Kerala. Literature — be it poetry or prose — was made popular by musicians, dancers and actors, both in simple village settings and in more sophisticated city theatres. The palaces and temples of Kerala fostered the evolution of musical traditions. Music was a form of worship and a way of spreading a message, and the poet-saints and royal composers (such as Swati Thirunal) added to its rich and vibrant treasure house.

Kathakali is believed to have originated over 1,500 years ago, blending the dramatic with the subtle, the masculine with the feminine. Themes are taken from the well-known myths of India (and, more recently, abroad, from tales taken from the *Iliad* and the Bible), with a cast rich in minor and major divinities, demons, kings and warriors. Percussion support from the native *chenda* and *maddalam* adds to the dramatic intensity of a performance, emphasising the exotic make-up and costumes and the exaggerated movements of the eyes and eyebrows. Traditionally, Kathakali is performed only by men, though today women are as expert dancers as men.

Mohiniattam or the dance of the enchantress, Mohini, is a womanly art, with soft swaying movements and delicate gestures. It combines the posture and facial expressiveness of Kathakali with the firm yet feminine techniques of Bharata Natyam.

Krishnanattam tells the stories of Lord Krishna, and is generally a form of worship. It is seen in its most pure form at the Shri Krishna temple at Guruvayur, and is performed over eight nights as a dance-drama.

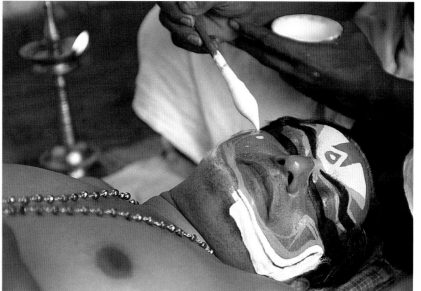

Theyyam or Thera has pagan echoes in its make-up, masks and movements, and is perhaps the oldest form of ritual dance from north Kerala — there are over 350 dances in the region. The Theyyam (a form or shape) depicts mythological, divine or heroic characters, and is associated with the Bhagavati cult, glorifying the goddess. It is performed exclusively by men wearing intricately-crafted costumes and accessories.

*T*he dance goes on: a
performer of Kudiyattam
(right), which is known
in the state as the dance
of antiquity. Women
dressed in traditional
Mohiniattam costumes of
linen and gold brocade
perform on stage (below).
Pages 32-33: *Arjuna
Nirittam at the Atham
celebrations at
Tirupunithura*

The musical instruments played for Theyyam include the *chenda*, *veekuchenda*, *elathalam* and *kuzhal*. Kudiyattam is another folk remnant from ancient times, a highly-evolved form of Koothu, and perhaps the only performing art form in Kerala that allowed participation by women. It is a theatrical presentation, introduced to the area by the Aryans thousands of years ago. A Kudiyattam performance traditionally takes place at night and can continue for many hours — or even days. The pivotal role belongs to the jester, who has the only speaking part and is the conduit between the actors and the audience.

Chavitunatakam is considered the Christian alternative to Kathakali. The actors speak, sing and stomp on the stage — in fact, a good performance was considered to be one during the course of which the floor was broken by the footwork! Themes are drawn

from medieval European history, and stories about Emperor Charlemagne are very popular !

With such a diversely ornamented heritage, the colours of Kerala are many-splendoured. Mural painting was perhaps the best and most prevalent of the plastic arts of Kerala, and covered the walls and ceilings of temples and palaces alike, telling stories of gods, goddesses and royalty. Tanjore and Mysore styles, influenced by European techniques, found expression in an uniquely 'Kerala' format, with brilliant colours and bold brush strokes — Raja Ravi Varma's oleographs and oil paintings are characteristic of this.

The festivals of the state are symbolic extravaganzas derived both from myth and from cross-settlements of civilisations from as far as Arabia and the West. The spirit of the land is given voice by the vibrant people who have created the unique culture of Kerala. The state — like most of India — celebrates a melange of festive occasions, dictated by religious affiliation and personal beliefs.

Onam is perhaps the most important celebration of the Malayali. Characteristic of the state's Hindu ethos, Onam is a harvest festival celebrating Kerala's New Year, at the end of the monsoon season, generally during August-September, or the Malayalam month of Chingam (the month of the lion). Onam is also identified with the homecoming of King Mahabali, who was vanquished by jealous gods, with the help of an avatar of Lord Vishnu: Vamana. It lasts four days, and is the story of good food, folk dances and bonhomie. Little mud pyramids are placed in the centre of circular floral arrangements, and young girls link their hands and dance around the *onakazhcha*. Traditionally, it is a day for gifts and feasting.

Navarathri is celebrated as Saraswati Puja in Kerala, where the goddess of learning and the arts is worshipped. Durgastami and Vijayadasami are observed as part of the nine-day-long period, which ends with the classic conquest of good over evil.

Sivarathri is celebrated in the Malayalam month of Kumbam (Aquarius) in February-March. The annual festival is traditionally held on the banks of the Periyar River at Alwaye. Makaravilakku, or the lighting of the many-tongued

lamp — most spectacular in Sabarimala — is the 41st and concluding day of the Mandalam season, which starts with the first day of the Malayalam month of Vrischikam (Scorpio) in November-December. Ashtami Rohini celebrates the birthday of Lord Krishna and is a part of Hindu ritual in the month of Chingam (Leo — August-September).

Christmas and Easter are the main festivals of the Christians. In addition, the Maramon Convention is held every year in March on the vast sandy bed of the Pamba river near Maramon, under the auspices of the Marthoma Church. It is said to be the biggest gathering of Christians in Asia.

The Muslims of Kerala celebrate various events in the Islamic calendar, as do Muslims all over the world. These include Bakr-id (Id-ul-Azhar) and Ramzan (Id-ul-Fitr), as well as Miladi Sherif (Nabi Dinam), which commemorates the birthday of the Prophet. In addition, the Chandanakunda at Beempally near Thiruvananthapuram is one of the most colourful Muslim festivals in Kerala. Lasting ten days and starting with the Jamadul Akbar of the Hajira year, it commemorates the death anniversary of Beema Beevi, a pious Muslim lady endowed

'Kerala cuisine might prove too spicy for a delicate palate,' warn tourist guides.

The spice trade in Kerala is about 7,500 years old. In fact, the Spice Coast, as the Malabar is called, is mentioned in ancient travelogues. Muziris (today's Crangannore or Kodungallur), where the Periyar flows into the sea, was once a rich port from where pepper was exported to foreign lands. Rome demanded prodigious amounts of spices, which came at a price that made the spice known as *karuthu ponnu*, or black gold. And there was no exchange possible — no Roman product was desired as much. Pliny is quoted as saying: 'The only quality of pepper is its pungency, and yet it is for this very undesirable element that we import it in very huge quantities.' It was paid for with gold — old Roman coins have been found in excavation sites in the state. Pepper was so highly prized that when Alaric the Goth laid siege to Rome in AD 408, he agreed to lift it only after he was paid off in 3,000 pounds of the spice!

New designs of ships were developed by the Etruscans, Greeks and Phoenicians, which allowed the lading of greater weights of cargo. In addition, the Arabs learned more about the monsoon winds and could use them to their maritime advantage. The whimsical tides of the Periyar caused the build-up of silt banks, which provided safe harbour for the ships that came into Muziris. Arabs, Turks, Venetians and the Chinese used the region as a port, and took with them vast amounts of pepper and other spices when they left — in fact, the Chinese legacy is still visible in the butterfly-like fishing nets, cooking vessels, umbrellas and firecrackers that the state is known for. But Muziris was soon abandoned for trade purposes and became a fort instead under the Portuguese, not just because it had become completely unusable with the accumulation of silt — Cochin took over in trading importance, with its well-developed harbour, and Calicut and Quilon became reputed ports too.

The fiery taste of pepper lured a large number of traders, who sped East in search of spices. The export volumes were enormous, and there was panic in Malabar. As one story goes, the natives ran to the Zamorin to complain: 'Sire!! We are in trouble! The Portuguese merchants are not just shipping away our pepper. They are uprooting and taking away the very pepper vines!'

The Zamorin smiled, and calmly said, 'Let them! Can the Portuguese take with them that last monsoon rain that gives the pepper its special flavour?'

Black pepper is a well-known preservative. Its Sanskrit name, *maricha*, means 'a particle of fire'. It has been used as a medicine and food flavouring for centuries. The pepper commonly used in cuisine is the dried form, with or without the outer cover. The Egyptians used it for embalming their dead, and in parts of Asia, it was considered to be an aphrodisiac. Some people also used it as an insect repellent. There are about 24 types of pepper grown in India, known by the area of their cultivation or origin, including Tellicherry or Alleppey pepper, and Penang or Singapore pepper. Kerala produces 98 per cent of India's pepper.

Cloves came to India just about 200 years ago. The Chinese were familiar with it, and it was customary to hold a clove in the mouth while addressing the king, to ensure that one's breath was sweet.

If pepper is the king of spices, the queen is cardamom. 'Grains of paradise' was the name given to these tiny seeds which lend their fragrant aroma and delicate taste to food and drink, perfumes and liquors from ancient times. While Kerala's pepper is famous worldwide, the cardamom the region produces is considered the best grown anywhere. In fact, today, only Kerala-grown cardamom is used for medicinal purposes in the West. Apart from its medicinal qualities, cardamom (*elettaria cardamomum*) enhances the flavour of beverages, confectionery, vegetarian and non-vegetarian food. It is grown primarily in the Idukki district in the Western Ghats, 750-1000 metres above sea level, in an area called the Cardamom Hills. India is the world's largest producer of cardamom, with Kerala contributing the largest share.

Salaam spices: Kerala attracted travellers from ancient Rome and Arabia, who were in quest of its spices. Cardamom being cleaned for the market (left), and the navadravyams, or the nine grains (above).

Canoes of time: the boat races at Aranmula, a centuries old, elaborate sporting event, which draws people from far and wide.

with extraordinary powers. On the last day of the festival, a procession led by caparisoned elephants precedes a display of fireworks.

In addition to religious celebrations, Kerala also hosts its own very special event, created and embellished especially for tourists. This is the time the giant mascot of the state — the elephant — comes into its own. Most festivals feature spectacular elephant processions; the Pooram and Vela are the best festivals when one can watch the tuskers in their caparisoned resplendence. Elephant pageants are usually accompanied by the Panchavadyam (the traditional five-instrument musical ensemble), Mohiniattam, Kathak and contemporary and folk dance forms. The events are generally held in the open-air theatre, Nishgandhi, in Thiruvananthapuram. The Thrissur Pooram is also

worth watching, with 30 elaborately decorated elephants marching to the beat of the *chendamelam*, accompanied by fireworks. It is held in April-May every year.

The Malayali, an enthusiastic festival addict, is generally dark-skinned and of average height. His traditional clothes were once made of linen and cotton, favouring white over other colours. Both men and women wore sarongs called *mundus*, with borders of thick gold brocade. The women were bare-breasted until the middle of the 20th century, with the exception of the Brahmins, who donned an upper covering. The wealthy covered their bosoms with ornaments and their backs with long hair, usually nourished by herbal oils and extract-of-flower shampoos. The traditional dress, typical of Hindu Malayali women is the *veshti* and *mundu* — an upper cloth worn over the sarong and the blouse, like a

half-sari. Young girls wore the *dhavani* and *pavaadai*, a colourful version of the *veshti*. But the invasion of the *salwar-kameez* has made the *dhavani-pavaadai* disappear completely, while the *mundu* and *veshti* is worn only on ceremonial occasions, favoured rarely by the young. Christian women have their own version of the *chatta* and *mundu*, with a fan-like arrangement at the back of the starched cotton, in the shape of a pleated tail. Muslim women too wore the *mundu*, but they also wore long-sleeved blouses called *rowkas*, buttoned up to the neck, with a coloured cloth over their heads. With the polarisation of

A boatful of bounty: fishermen prepare for their day on a warm summer morning, getting the vanchis (boats) ready (above); succulent oysters from the deep (left).

religion, they have today retreated behind the burka, which used to be a rare sight in Kerala until about the 1970s.

It is important to know the geography of the land if you want to understand the changes it has gone through. The legends of Kerala were once kept alive by travelling bards called *panans*, who composed and sang stories of battles and lovers, kings and tyrants. Kerala is predominantly an agricultural society, and rice, coconut, rubber and tapioca are the most important field crops, which together account for over half its arable area. Other important field crops are ginger, pineapple, cashew, pod vegetables and legumes such as beans, chickpeas and pigeon peas, and a variety of spices. Kerala has long been famous for growing pepper, as we know. It also produces about 95 per cent of the nation's rubber. Commercial poultry farming is highly developed. In the central part of the state, between the coast and the inland plateau, commercially important trees are the cashew, jackfruit, mango and palm.

N et of plenty: a typical idyllic scene on the backwaters and lakes of Kerala; a fisherman casting his net from his boat.

Time is the great healer, they say, and the route along which Kerala travels, takes a rest with the ancient system of healing known as ayurveda.

It is said to have been developed around 600 BC and emphasised not just the cure, but methods of prevention of various ailments. Practised today all over India and abroad, ayurveda is a holistic treatment that focusses on achieving an optimal balance of bodily humours, to create a healthy individual. In Kerala, ayurveda has its own special forms, shaped by the environment, raw materials available, and the practitioners' style of treatment.

The general techniques of massage, with oil baths (*pizhichil*), leaf bundles (*ilakkizhi*), rice packs (*navara*), containing specific herbs and dipped in warm oil (*navarakizhi*), or one of several other methods, are widely and effectively used in cases of chronic and severe problems, including rheumatoid arthritis, paralysis, facial palsy, spondylitis, polyneuritis, spinal problems, gastric or peptic ulcers.

The best time to undergo a course of ayurvedic treatment, it is believed, is during the monsoon (June to November), when the air is comparatively dust-free and cool, allowing the body to open all its pores and become ideally receptive to the therapeutic power of the powders and oils used. There are several well-known clinics and health-care centres that have been established in various parts of the state that offer special packages for general well-being and specific ailments. In fact, expert masseurs and ayurveda specialists have now established centres all over the country and worldwide, where they practise and teach techniques perfected over time.

The magic of herbs: the healing science of ayurveda has been practised in Kerala for centuries, and today is a great magnet for tourists who go there in search of rejuvenation. Sirodhara (right) being carried out by a physician.

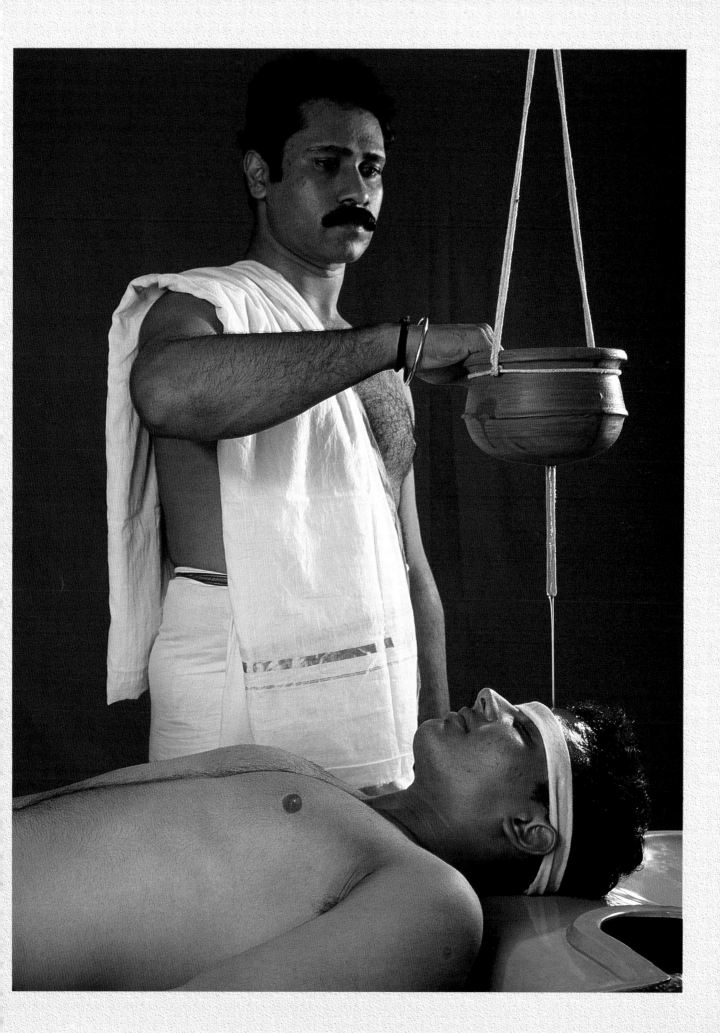

Forests cover a quarter of the land area of Kerala — bamboo, ebony, rosewood and teak. The woodlands are also a source of charcoal, resin and wood pulp. Coconut groves cover most of the coastal lowlands of the state, and the nuts are an indispensible part of the Malayali way of life. The locals make ropes and matting from coir (made from coconut fibre). They use coconut oil to make soap and cosmetics, extract the meat (kernel) for food, and feed the oil cake — left over from squeezing out the oil from the dried kernel or copra — to livestock. In the past, hollowed-out trunks of coconut palms were used to make canoes. People still use the leaves of coconut palms to thatch houses, weave baskets, make brooms, fans and umbrellas, and as fuel. The coconut flower is an important ingredient in the alcoholic beverage called toddy, and also in vinegar. Kerala's rubber plantations are on the lower slopes of the state's highlands. The same area also has coffee, pepper, tea and cardamom plantations. Ginger, pepper, cardamom, cinnamon, cloves, vanilla, turmeric, nutmeg, cumin, garlic and star anise are exported to other parts of India and the world. Thekaddy is a major spice-growing area, as are Murikkady, Vandiperiyar and Vandanmedu — one of the world's largest cardamom auction arenas. Kumily is a spice-trade centre.

While land reform brought about by the Communists in the 1950s transferred land ownership to the landless, it also ensured the passing of government patronage of the arts to the Marxists. This simultaneously sharpened the caste divide in Kerala, with politicised Ezhavas and their SNDP forming a large vote base for the

Communists, while the Nairs and others stood by the Congress. The empowerment of the lower castes and classes revolutionised Kerala society, but had its downside too. Art and culture, according to Leftist intellectual diktat, had to be people-oriented, rather than culturally authentic. This was food for thought.

Travelling through Kerala is also a culinary journey — Kerala cuisine is second to

Water vistas: a breathtaking view — a river rushes down the Western Ghats (left), and the backwaters at Kasaragode (below).

none. The vast paddy fields, coconut groves, vegetable gardens, fruit orchards and spice plantations aplenty provide the ingredients for an array of delicious dishes. Most homes rear milch cattle and poultry, while the treasure trove that is the sea, and its various feeder channels, is within easy reach. All this, along with the diverse population of the coastal state, has resulted in a wide variety of foods, native to the region. In addition, good transport systems and the characteristic Malayali acceptance of external customs — from the wheat and corn of the Punjab to the spices and cooking methods of Gujarat — has influenced the food habits of the local people.

Typically, Kerala cuisine is strongly flavoured, sour and chilli hot. Rice is a staple, along with other starchy products such as yams, tapioca and cassava. These are livened up with spicy curries and stews made with vegetables, fish or meat, often cooked with coconut or coconut milk.

Apart from coconut, chillies and turmeric, popular additions to any recipe are leaves of different kinds (neem, coriander, mint), and spices (ginger, cardamom, cloves, pepper, etc.). Yoghurt, tamarind or a form of *kokum* are used to give a sour taste to the food. Vegetables are favoured, from the roots and tubers of yams, cassava, tapioca, sweet potatoes and carrots, to the many varieties of spinach, drumsticks,

*A*rt of time: a 12th-century wood carving in Sasthan Kulangarai Temple at Chengannur near Kottayam (above); lamp-makers (right), and bronze sculpture at Kunnimangalam (above right)

beans, gourds, cabbage, cauliflower, radish, raw and ripe bananas and plantains. Jackfruit — both raw and ripe — and breadfruit are also widely eaten.

Both meat and fish are eaten in the form of curries and are also sautéed or fried. Beef, mutton, pork, chicken and duck are widely available, as are mackerel, sardine, catfish, tuna, and a variety of fresh and salt-water fish and shellfish. A number of vegetables, meats and fish are pickled in a pungent blend of spices and sour sauces, eaten with less spiced rice and lentil dishes, or with yoghurt or yoghurt-based concoctions.

Kerala cuisine is also governed by religious affiliation. The Hindus, or Chakyars, who belong to the Namboodri Brahmin class, were given the right as per the Shastras to cook for the temple and its residents. They produced food that conformed to the Shastras, and contained all the elements: sweet, sour, pungent, salty, bitter and astringent, with variations in texture. This was vegetarian cuisine, with typical recipes including *parippu*, *erusseri*, *puliserri*, *pachadi*, *kalam*, *olan*, *thoren*, *thiyal*, *upperi*, *ingipuli*, and more. *Payasam*, or the pudding, is made with rice, milk, coconut milk, jaggery, jackfruit and banana. Boiled or parboiled and hand-pounded rice is a staple, and red rice

(unpolished) is believed to be a healthy alternative. The vegetarian medley that is *avial* is considered by the traditional to be a modern innovation.

Syrian Christian cooking has a strong Hindu bias, but is influenced to a great extent by Syrian, Dutch, Portuguese and British missionaries who settled in the region. It is very similar to the Sinhalese cuisine of Sri Lanka, with the extensive use of fish, red chillies and a souring agent called *kudampuli*, which balances flavours, acts as an antiseptic and has anti-allergic properties. The cooking medium is generally coconut oil, and coconut is commonly used in its various forms. Favourite foods include hoppers (*appams*), *puttu*, *kanji*, stews, *irachi olathiyathu*, banana, breadfruit, yam, tapioca, steamed or boiled jackfruit and shrimp.

The Moplahs, or local Muslims, are the descendants of Arab traders who married the women of the area. Their cuisine is strongly influenced by the flavours of Arabia, with the extensive use of wheat in *pattiri* (chapatis). Rice and coconut are common to the diet of both Hindus and Muslims. Beef and mutton, as well as chicken and seafood, are favourites, used in spicy *pulaos* and biryanis.

*T*he deity of the forest: Ayyappan (above) is one of the Malayali's favourite deities, and Sabarimala is one of Kerala's holiest places. It is situated in the heart of the forest, on top of the Sashtha mountain. Devotees undergo penance for weeks before starting on their pilgrimage, and children pose at a studio with Ayyappan cutouts (left).

Fishing is a major industry along Kerala's extensive coastline and about a quarter of India's total fish catch comes from there. The state exports a number of marine products, especially frozen shrimp. Local farmers use fish waste as a fertiliser. Kerala has a variety of mineral deposits, including white clay. The sandy beaches of southern Kerala are rich in the main ore of titanium. Rich ores of thorium and other rare elements are also found there.

Wild pink water lilies fringe the green mirrors of village ponds and small temple tarns. Vermilion roads stretch into the sunset, punctuated by swaying bullock carts laden with hay, golden in the twilight, with lanterns swaying on their undersides, brightening the passage into the darkness which invades the land. Dusk in Kerala has an atmosphere of legend, an unreality which has not been completely obliterated by STD booths, internet cafes, concrete housing and modern storefronts. The state has a high literacy rate, with widespread female education, a low infant death rate, high longevity and more such positive statistics, especially in comparison with the more advanced countries of the world. In fact, Kerala is a model of low productivity and high living standards, created by better distribution of wealth and high literacy levels. In some ways, the region can be considered to be one single urban centre with fairly efficient transport and communication facilities. Women are generally better educated than their counterparts in many other parts of India, and they enjoy a highly respected position in society. Historically speaking, the matrilineal system was predominant; now, however, nuclear families are far more common. But even today, in traditional society, combined matrilineal households of fifty or more members are found. Farming is one of the main sources of income. Salaries from employment in the Arabian Gulf also contributed considerably to the prosperity of the state some years ago, though this has declined considerably over the past decade or so. The Gulf boom created a major change in Kerala's social structure and architecture. In the 1970s, concrete architecture came into vogue in many places, with the returning immigrants from the Gulf acquiring importance in the area as a

Kalaripayattu is the source of judo, karate and other Asian styles of combat. It is practised even today, as a sport, with two combatants armed with swords and shields.

result of their wealth. But the 90s have seen a return to the traditional architecture, *thachusastra*, whose main exponents are to be found among the Namboodris of Thrissur.

Most of Kerala's inhabitants speak Malayalam. Some of India's least modern tribal clans live in the hill regions of Kerala, perhaps related to the Veddas, the nomadic woodland folk native to Sri Lanka. Others may be the descendants of the region's first human inhabitants; they are called Adivasis, a generic term for aboriginals. The de-Sanskritisation of the language and sensibility came much later, in the late 70s, with Marxist-Dravidianism, which thought that art and language had to be de-Brahminised, and therefore de-Aryanised. But then, there are famous Namboodri writers like Kattumadom Narayanan, who deny that their Brahminism has anything to do with the Aryan putsch south of the Vindhyas, and that there were Dravidian Brahmins from ancient times, living in Kerala. Education is more advanced in Kerala than in many other parts of India. Over 90 per cent of the people can read and write. By law, boys and girls must attend school between the ages of six and 14, and school attendance is almost 100 per cent. The state has about 12,000 schools, 200 colleges and five universities.

Kerala has a flourishing local press, with six daily newspapers and an English-language magazine published in the state. These publications have contributed considerably to the high literacy standards and social awareness of the Malayali community in India and abroad.

The origin of Malayalam as a separate and distinct language can be traced to about the 9th century AD, as the last Dravidian linguistic tradition to take concrete shape. It had its root in Tamil, but was subsequently influenced by Sanskrit and Prakrit, developing its own script and a rich literary store of its own. Poetry flourished under royal patronage for many centuries, with descriptive and narrative verse finding large and enthusiastic audiences. Over the years, this poetic exposition became

associated with expressive techniques such as Kathakali and Krishnanattam, performed on stage, which served to educate as well as entertain. Portuguese missionaries brought the printing press to the region in the 19th and 20th centuries, and dictionaries and other reference works were produced. The reign of Raja Swati Thirunal was perhaps the most prolific for poems and songs, the ruler himself being an accomplished composer. Malayalam poetry became less content-oriented and played with diction and word games for a while, until inspiration gave it new life, with strong flavours from the West providing fresh ideas. Novels and short stories also used real life as their source of inspiration, and the themes ranged from the historical to the moral. Essays, scientific writings, travelogues and biographies also formed a part of the vast repertoire of talent from the region.

Everything to do with Kerala is somehow imbued with a trace of a particular

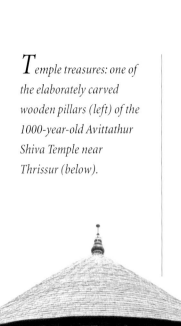

Temple treasures: one of the elaborately carved wooden pillars (left) of the 1000-year-old Avittathur Shiva Temple near Thrissur (below).

myth, as if a culture confronting modern ideologies and practices had to create an enchantment of its own, where it could retreat. And if you are looking for myth with valet parking, that too is available.

You could stay at the resorts in Kumarakom, where old houses (*tharavads*) have been transplanted beside calm lagoons, with bathrooms open to the sky. Kumarakom, 'discovered' barely a decade ago, is a backwater lagoon with a spectacular view and a 14-acre bird sanctuary, where ducks, cuckoos, Siberian storks and other species are regular visitors. Enterprising locals have converted traditional covered canoes (*kettuvallam*) into luxury houseboats that attract tourists from all over the world.

You can take a houseboat and drift along the backwaters, watching the glimmering reflections in the water, the silvery trail of passage behind, like a postscript, and hear the birds call out across the treetops. In Travancore and Kochi, you can feast on spiced tapioca and fish, duck curry or beef sautéed with coconut strips. Creating an aqueous web through the slim silhouette of landscape that is

*C*hurchcraft: *Murals behind the main altar in St. George's Orthodox Church at Paliakara near Tiruvalla (left); the Basilica of Our Lady of Dolours at Thrissur (below); and (right) the granite cross, known as the Persian Cross in Kottayom Valiyapally (St. Mary's Kaanaya Church)*

Kerala is the vast lattice of canals, lagoons, lakes and rivers, known generally as the backwaters. These have been formed by over 40 small and large rivers that flow west into the Indian Ocean. They once stretched right across the area; many of these channels are now closed by siltation, but are gradually being reclaimed to realise their true worth, both as trade routes and as popular tourist attractions.

The backwaters are the living museums of rural Kerala, where the traditional way of life still survives. It is highly labour-intensive, with the local people engaged in country-boat building, prawn cultivation, sand mining, coir manufacture, underwater limestone collection, rice cultivation and duck farming.

Kerala's cultural activities and scenic beauty attract many visitors. Most tourists come from other Indian states, but the influx of foreign visitors has increased

*G*ods on earth: the architecture of Kerala's temples is unique, with carved pillars and tiled, gabled roofs. The Peruvanam Mahadeva Temple near Thrissur (previous page), and the Sree Padmanabha Swami Temple at Thiruvananthapuram (left) are typical examples; wood carvings in the 100-year-old Avittathur Shiva Temple near Thrissur (above and below).

considerably over the past few years. Tourists are drawn to the comfortable climate and the exotic wildlife of the state. The coastlands support gulls and cranes and are an ideal habitat for a large number of migratory species. The forests of the interior are inhabited by bisons, elephants, panthers and tigers.

The best season for tourism is August to March. A typical backwater journey begins at Alappuzha (or Alleppey, dubbed the Venice of the East), and winds through the small canals into Vembanad Lake. The area around the lake is called Kuttanad, and was once known as the rice bowl of Kerala. Kuttanad is actually below sea level, and paddy fields have been created by an ingenious system of dykes and bunds, which ensure that the arable areas maintain optimum moisture and temperature levels.

Kollam, Kayamkulam Lake and Ashtamudi Lake are also worth a visit, as are Veli (in south Kerala), Kadinamkulam, Edava,

At sea: Anwatirtha Beach near Kasaragode

Anjengo, Madayara, Peravur, Kodungallur, Chetuva and Valiyaparamba (in north Kerala).

During the monsoon, the backwaters host the traditional snake-boat races, featuring the 130-feet long *chundan valloms*. These were believed to have been originally designed for ancient naval battles fought in the region. Local chieftains of the then kingdoms of Vadakkumkoor (northern kingdom), Thekkumkoor (southern kingdom) and Chempakassery maintained their *chundan valloms* as a means of defence against the marauding enemy. Today they attract the click of thousands of cameras and cheering crowds from all over the world. It is considered an honour to win — or to have supported the team that does — and the reward prized most is the fame, not the money!

The chief rivers of Kerala are the Periyar, the Pamba and the Bharathapuzha. Their rapid flow has allowed them to be harnessed for hydroelectric schemes, but the generation of electricity has not always been reliable. Where the rivers flow into the sea, sandbanks have been formed, which protect the coast from the ravages of the Arabian Sea. These provide safe anchorage for small vessels using Kerala's minor sea ports. Artificial cuts (canals) link the coastal lagoons. The Vembanad Lake, a large body of water, is an enlarged lagoon.

The rivers gleam through clearings in the trees; their silver sands were once tournament arenas for warriors of yesteryear.

If you come across two young men duelling with flashing swords and clashing spears, their brown bodies gleaming with oil, and their cummerbunds red, like blood, you will feel that you have stepped into another time — you are seeing *kalaripayattu*, an ancient art of warfare. History dimly records the travels of a Buddhist warrior monk who travelled from Kerala to Tibet and China during the time of Sankaracharya. The

martial arts of Kerala are as eye-catching as the more refined dance forms of the region — almost balletic, they were developed by warriors, who fought with sticks and swords, and were a formidable force. *Kalaripayattu* is the oldest, most scientific and comprehensive system of martial training in the world, believed to be the source of traditions such as judo, karate and other Asian styles of combat. Its origins can be traced to the 12th century AD, when soldiers were taught in a *kalari* or training ground. Medical and massage techniques are used to make the body supple and agile, discipline is intense, and the wounds received during classes, even today, are real.

The Parisakali of north Malabar and the semi-religious Velakali of Travancore are martial art forms which involve considerable physical exertion and training in the use of weapons. The second form is supposed to have been used in the battle between the Pandavas and the Kauravas at Kurukshetra.

All this was before the first prophet of Hinduism, Adi Sankara, born in Kaladi beside the river Bharathapuzha, began his long journey towards Badrinath. Myth and fable are

Ancient legacy: fishing boats docked at sunset in Port Kochi. In the background is the famous filigree of Chinese fishing nets.

*P*achyderm paradise:
wild elephants in their
natural habitat in the
popular Thekkady
national park

Kerala style: a proud owner in the contemporary Malayali garb of shirt and sarong dismounts from his elaborately painted lorry.

entwined with the legends of the land. Centuries ago, another warrior monk, Parasurama, was supposed to have flung his battle axe into the sea to carve out the land of Kerala from the ocean. And ironically, if you travel to the birthplace of Parasurama, beside a lake called Renuka in the foothills of the Himalayas, the vegetation is surprising — the lake is fringed with palm trees.

Kerala's temples have their own special architecture with the huge 'flagpole' in the centre, and the gabled roof which covers the quadrangle of the building. The temple pagodas have intricate carvings of deities, illustrating legends and myths. Hindus form the largest religious group in Kerala, and comprise about half the state's population. Christians and Muslims account for the rest, with a small minority of Jains, Buddhists and Jews. The Namboodris of Kerala were considered the highest caste, and topped a hierarchy governed by very strict norms and codes of behaviour. Below them came the non-Malayali Brahmins, the Kshatriyas or warriors, and the Ambalavasis or temple servants. Trade and business, traditionally a Vaishya realm, was controlled by the Syrian Christians, Muslims, Jews and non-Malayalis. The Nairs, a soldier class, were Sudras, while the 'polluting' castes consisted of the Ezhavas or untouchable peasants, toddy tappers and coconut growers. In 1936, Travancore opened its Hindu temples to all Hindu worshippers, regardless of their caste and class. Cochin followed suit in 1948.

Legend has it that the Namboodris were the original inhabitants of Kerala, brought in by Parasurama to populate the land he had carved out from the sea with his axe. Ironically, they were also among the first converts to Christianity!

The Christian faith is believed to have oriental origins. According to one school of thought, the church founded by St. Thomas (before he was killed by a Brahmin in Madras) predates the Roman religious base. But actually the chronicle starts with the

arrival of Cana Thomas of Syria, who arrived with his followers in AD 345; the two groups blended and the Syrian Christian system of belief grew. However, when the Portuguese came to Kerala in 1498, they forcibly converted the local Christians to their form of Latin-style worship. When the Dutch took over control in 1663, life became easier for the original Syrian Christians, who had Syro-Chaldean priests. The Anglicans also exerted their influence when the English reigned supreme in the region about a 100 years later. Today, Christianity in Kerala is a medley of many forms of the faith, interpreted in a way that is unique to the state and its people; for instance, every newborn in a Syrian Christian family has a horoscope cast — a very Hindu custom!

Islam came with the spice trade. Arabs married the local women and the resulting population converted to Islam — they were called the Moplahs, or Mappilas. Their culture and customs are a remarkable blend of Indian and Arab traditions.

Most ancient civilisations flourished where there was water, since it was the most efficient form of transport at that time. Kerala was ideally situated from this point of view, and developed a great and enduring culture, influenced in part by invaders down the ages. In addition, the state's own natural resources, from the spices and forests to the people and their customs, make it a unique region.

Cattle thunder: cattle racing is an old Kerala sport, attended once by kings and commoners alike. Two racers coax their oxen through mud and slush at a race near Kollam.

A rock inscription dating from the reign of Emperor Ashoka — who ruled India around 200 BC — refers to the Chera people, in what could be the first historical mention of Kerala as a distinct region in India. The area was ruled by the Chera dynasty until about AD 400. Traders from as far away as Rome exchanged gold coins for pepper and other spices, muslin, sandalwood, ivory and various exotic products of the land. During this period, Hinduism, Buddhism, and Jainism were introduced to South India by monks and migrants. St. Thomas, the Christian apostle, is believed to have founded the 'Syrian' Church at Muziris (Crangannore, today's Kodungallur) before AD 100. Jewish migrants established a settlement in Cochin around AD 900.

After the decline of the Chera dynasty, 200 years of confusion followed. During this time, Islam was brought to Kerala by Arab merchants. In AD 825, the Kulasekhara dynasty began a new calendar, founded the city of Quilon, and set Kerala on a new path to a progressive future. Over the next 200 years, Malayalam developed as a separate language, which was close to but distinct from Tamil. Arts and learning flourished. Then, a 100 years of conflict with the Cholas, from what is now Tamil Nadu, destroyed Kerala's prosperity and split the region into smaller, constantly warring states. Ravi

Varma Kulasekhara, a local ruler, established a short-lived empire, but his sudden death in 1314 caused Kerala to fall apart once more into pockets of hostility.

However, all through the turbulent times, trade flourished with the rest of the world. Muziris (Kodungallur) was the most important commercial port. Quilon and Calicut were also prosperous trading centres. The sea-faring civilisations of the ancient world — the Phoenicians, Greeks, Arabs, Romans — made these towns their destinations or transit points en route to the Far East. Spice was the reason these maritime voyagers took so many risks and travelled across the seas to a land that was, for them, unfamiliar.

During the middle ages, the Arabs attained monopoly over the trade and the markets, and blocked off all land and sea routes to the East. This forced the Europeans — Portuguese and Spaniards mainly — to find an alternate passage. Most sailed around the coast of Africa. But Christopher Columbus was more adventurous — he reasoned that if the world was indeed round, as had more or less been agreed upon by then, he could go west and reach the same destination eventually. Sponsored by the Spanish court, his epic journey took him to the Americas. So, in a way, it was while looking for Kerala that the New World was discovered!

In 1488, the Portuguese — in a ship captained by Bartolomeu Dias — landed on the southern coast of Africa, which they called 'The Cape of Storms'. Later, as the conviction grew that it was a good way to get to the East, the name was changed to the 'Cape of Good Hope'.

On July 8, 1497, a Portuguese expedition under Vasco da Gama set out from Lisbon, rounded the Cape of Good Hope (November 22), and reached Calicut on May 20, 1498. On December 25, 1500, the Portuguese navigator Pedro Alvares Cabral arrived and began the Portuguese domination of trade on the Malabar coast. The Dutch pushed out the Portuguese in the 1600s, but were themselves decisively eliminated in 1741 by King Martanda Varma of Travancore, who unified the region. However, between 1766 and 1790, invasions from Mysore, led by Hyder Ali and Tipu Sultan, successfully fragmented the empire once again.

After the death of Tipu Sultan in 1792, Britain's East India Company annexed Malabar. Treaties brought the states of Travancore and Cochin under their control too. But rebellion made the period unstable and uncertain. Pazhassi Raja of Malabar led a

*S*miling sylph: once her ancestors roamed the forests and glades of Kerala's forestland and wooded hillslopes. But today, this tribal girl, dressed in modern clothes, smiles for the camera.

five-year revolt against British rule, which ended with his execution in 1805. Another uprising under Velu Thampi of Travancore also ended with his execution in 1809. The Moplahs rose in rebellion from 1849 to 1855, and again in 1921.

But British rule was not all-oppressive and unhappy. It was also marked by the establishment of an effective education system and the extension of plantation agriculture, especially tea. The rulers improved facilities at Cochin, as a major port, and set up a network of communications, including better links with the rest of India, which eventually became the basis for development after Indian independence in 1947.

The evolution of Kerala as a democratic state was first expressed through social reform, the most influential of its proponents being Narayana Guru, who believed in 'one caste, one religion, one God for mankind'. The Communists, on the one hand, played an important role in the anti-colonial movement in Kerala, spearheaded by people like K.P. Kesava Menon, A.K. Pillai, E.M.S. Namboodripad, K. Kesavan, T.M. Varghese, P. Krishna Pillai, and A.K. Gopalan. In 1947, the Communists organised armed insurrections against the state of Travancore in the villages of Vayalar and Punnapra.

Independence from British colonial rule came on August 15, 1947. Two years later, in 1949, the two separate states of Travancore and Cochin were united. In 1956, the boundaries of the newly united states were revised to include neighbouring Malayalam-speaking areas, and the whole territory was officially named Kerala.

The state's political history since 1956 has been troubled, with rival parties holding power for short periods of time, punctuated by interludes of President's rule. The Communist Party, which broke the monopoly of the local ruling Congress Party in 1957, has proven itself to be restrained but effective in government. However, coalition politics is more Kerala's game, given the large numbers of political factions with varying ideologies. Kerala has 20 elected members in the Lok Sabha (lower house) and nine nominated representatives in the Rajya Sabha (upper house) of the Indian National Parliament. The state government is led by a governor and a chief minister. The state legislative assembly has 140 elected members and one nominated member, and the state and central governments and semi-government institutions are the largest employers, accounting for about 80 per cent of the total employment available. Many work for Kerala's 21 state-owned manufacturing companies. Others find employment in education, health care and other services. Manufacturing does not constitute a major revenue earner for the state. This is possibly a result of intense unionisation. Communism, in trying to indigenise international revolution, succeeded in creating stringent union practices which discourage industrial investments. Though the tendency to call strikes by unions have became less in the 21st century, Kerala has lost thousands of man years in industral development. However, the state government has set up about 12,000 factories, employing approximately 300,000 people. The products of these factories include aluminium, cement, ceramics, petroleum and petro-chemicals, titanium, rare earths, pharmaceuticals, insecticides, electrical equipment, fertilisers, glass, hand-woven textiles, matches, paper, pencils, plywood, synthetic fibres, telephone cables, transformers and veneers. The processing of sugar and tea are also fairly important. Traditional industrial practices include the

processing of cashews and coconuts, and weaving. Coconuts have long been used to produce fibres, soaps and cosmetics. Traditional large-scale crafts still surviving in Kerala include the making of furniture, mats, pottery, rattan work, brass and leather goods, and handicrafts.

The roads of Kerala have been traversed by people bringing with them their diverse cultures, as when Rome ruled the western world, and the Moors took with them shiploads of cloves and cardamoms to satisfy Roman palates. To the Kerala coast, the Arabs brought Islam, and until the Portuguese arrived, lived in harmony with the natives, under the benevolent protection of its kings. They became the sailors of Kerala's navies, and famous admirals like the Marakkars defeated the Portuguese in battles. From Kozhikode to Kannur, the coast of northern Kerala flaunts its almost medieval skyline with its innumerable turreted forts.

From its southern seaside tip to its northern mountains, it doesn't take very long to travel across the state. But it is a journey into history and an idyllic, magical world — a haven for all who seek a quiet and tranquil interlude, away from the hustle and bustle of the world.

Street nymphs: village girls busy with their morning chores (above); Pookkolam: *floral decoration for Onam celebration (below).*
Pages 78-79: *Kozhikode beach*

The author wishes to thank Ramya Sarma
for her invaluable editorial help and research,
which have contributed greatly to the
substance of this book.

❋

ISBN: 81-7436-161-8

© Roli Books Pvt. Ltd., 2001
Lustre Press Pvt. Ltd.
M-75, Greater Kailash II (Market)
New Delhi 110 048, India.
Phones: (011) 6442271, 6462782, 6460886
Fax: (011) 6467185, E-mail: roli@vsnl.com
Website: rolibooks.com

Text: Ravi Shankar

Photographs: V. Muthuraman

Other photographs:
Amit Pasricha: pp. 3 (bottom), 18-19, 24, 29,
33 (bottom), 47 (top right)
Anil Mehrotra: p. 3 (top)
M. Balan: pp. 6-7, 51, 68-69, 74-75
Salim Pushpnath: pp. 26-27, 33 (top), 45,
46-47 (top left and bottom left)
Usha Kris: pp. 55 (top), 44 (bottom)

Design: Inkspot

Printed and bound in Singapore